IF I SHOULD DIE
IF I SHOULD LIVE

written by Joanne Marxhausen

art by Benjamin Marxhausen

Publishing House
St. Louis

to Jesus, who lives in me

Concordia Publishing House, St. Louis, Missouri

Copyright © 1975 Concordia Publishing House
Manufactured in the United States of America

Library of Congress Cataloging in Publication Data

Marxhausen, Joanne.
    If I should die, if I should live.

    SUMMARY: Examines death from the prespective of
the Christian who looks forward to everlasting life.
    1. Death—Juvenile literature. [1. Death]
I. Marxhausen, Benjamin. II. Title.
BT825.M34   236'.1   75-11648
ISBN: 0-570-03440-X   Hardbound
ISBN: 0-570-07793-1   Paperback

4 5 6 7 8 9 10 11 12 SB 89 88 87 86 85 84 83 82 81

A long time ago

God decided I should live.

I was born.

I walk
  and talk.

I sing
  and laugh.

I work,

I play.

Sometimes I cry.

And sometimes I do things
that God doesn't like.

God said,

"Whoever does bad things

must die . . .

FOREVER!"

That would hurt very bad!

I would never sing and laugh.

There would be nothing but crying,

and it would never end!

But God is
so full of love

He wants everyone

to live . . .

. . . FOREVER.

So God decided

Jesus should live

and show people

how much God loves them.

Jesus was born.

He walked
and talked.

He sang
and laughed.

He worked,
He played.

Sometimes He cried.

But He never did anything
God didn't like.

Jesus lived a perfect life

for all people . . .

. . . even me!

And God decided

Jesus should die

for all people . . .

. . . even me!

So Jesus died.

But Jesus was really God,
and He didn't die forever. . . .

JESUS LIVES AGAIN!

Now Jesus lives inside me

so that if I should die

it won't be forever.

When I die I will just

stop living on this earth

and I will

live again

in heaven.

It will be so

nice in heaven!

Think of the most beautiful

sight in the world.

Heaven is even more beautiful . . .

. . . so beautiful

no one can even imagine it!

Think of the brightest color there is.

Heaven is even brighter . . .

. . . and it won't ever get dark!

Think of the happiest thing
that could ever happen.

Heaven is even happier . . .

. . . and no one will ever cry there!

Think of the most peaceful time
you have ever known.

Heaven is even

more peaceful . . .

. . . there will never be war there . . .

nothing can ever go wrong there

. . . no one will be lonely

or afraid there . . .

. . . ever!

Think of the most fun
you could ever have.

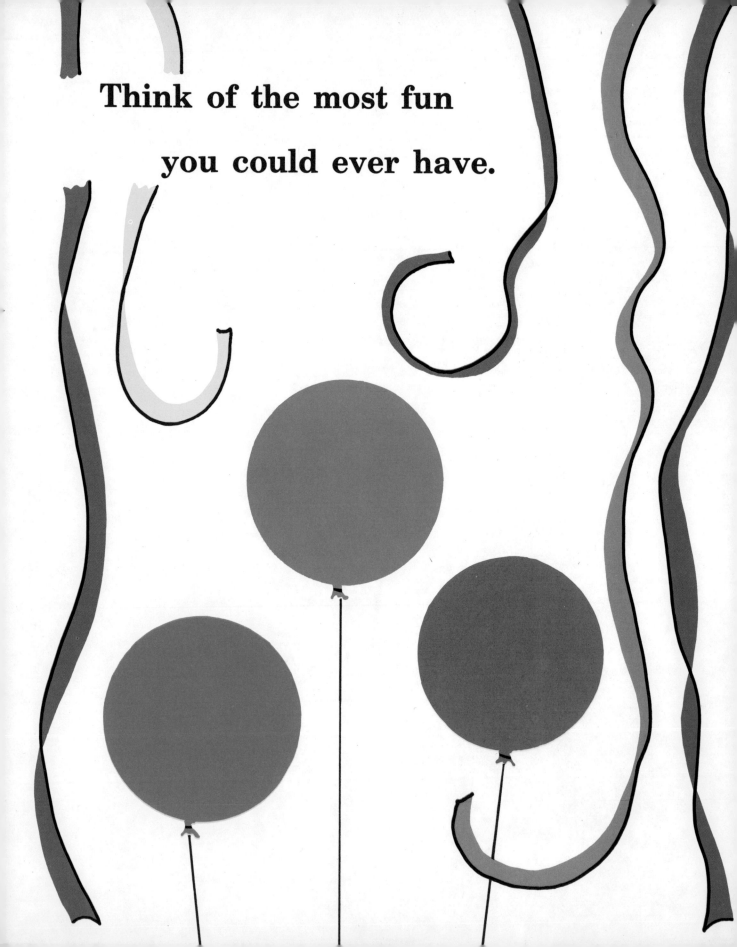

Heaven is more fun . . .

and it will last

FOREVER!

God will decide when I should die,
and the time will be
just right . . .

. . . because God is very wise.

If I should die very soon,

I will be glad—

then I will live

in this bright and beautiful

happiness that will never end

and I will see Jesus!

But maybe God has decided

that I should live

here on this earth yet

for a long, long time.

God said, "With Jesus living in you
you can have a little bit
of heaven's peace and
happiness right now.

All you have to do is . . . love."

I do want to be happy

until I should die,

so Jesus will help me love

if I should live.